BEWARE THE MEDIOCRITY

A Poetry Collection

By
Mia Guiliano

Mia Guiliano

Beware the Mediocrity

Copyright © 2018

All rights reserved

Typeset by: Digital Content Creators

Website: www.digitalcc.us

Table of Contents

Beware the Mediocrity	1
Betrayal	2
Fire	3
What is Right	4
Stars	5
The Tale of Fame	6
Perfection	7
To Be a Leader	8
Remembering the Future	9
Reality	10
Footprints	11
Way Back Now	12
Fireflies	13
Soft as Rock	14
Deep Mirrors	15
Exceptional Fear	17
Freedom	19
Careless	21
Dreams	22
A Story	24
Acknowledgements	26
About the Author	27

BEWARE THE MEDIOCRITY

Beware the Mediocrity
That shadows all the clones
All the same, scared of fame
Giving in to sighs and groans

Betrayal

I want others to do well
Yet never more than me
Is this betrayal something I should tell
Or is it something they already see?

FIRE

Empty void of souls far black
Flickering, waiting to shine
Seeps light through darkness' crack
This fire, this flame of mine

A soft warmth hard as rock
Burns and scatters to form light
Welcome sight to chain and lock
To burn through wood, flame must fight

Twisting turning, embers in a soul
Turn light to dark, wood to strong fire
Feed fear and courage, fill the empty hole
A unsolved ache you must inspire

WHAT IS RIGHT

What is right and what is true
Are they aware of what they do
They get away with all they say
A ruthless killing of their prey

The harm they do to me and you
Told lies and truths that are not true
It may be wrong to say they are strong
The carnage has gone on too long

They believe that they are power
And get scared when we don't cower
Tear us down letter by letter
Why let them think that they are better

Told a thousand times that we are weak
Strength and power we cannot seek
Get shoved aside, forced to hide
And yet we say our hands are tied

Stars

What a feeling of alone can do
Separated by a veil of shun
Surrounded by people, none talking to you
Of thousands you are one

Lost in a crowd thick full of others
Hidden talents and voices
Noticed by only fathers and mothers
Not noticeably bolder with each of our choices

Standing up screaming with all of our being
Shouts and cries form a river of longing
Still us no one is seeing,
Craving that feeling of belonging

One future ahead we will go far
The quiet, the brave, and unnoticed we are
Trapped souls encased in a pretty glass jar
Each a lone beautiful star

The Tale of Fame

Alas now me they agonize
Later they'll apologize
When I become rich and wise
I hope I may see through the lies

Scared beyond truth can say
Then anger in a moments day
And of course my heart begins to swell
Knowing hatred more than they can tell

I'll live like kings of old
Disprove all they have foretold
For now alone am I, and cold
Awaiting my crown of pain and gold

What I would become they never knew
And yet with them I truly grew
For a tale of fame lacks in truth
If not the hero were mocked in youth

PERFECTION

An image of perfection
That scares me each time we meet
An ever present fear of rejection
From someone inside and out sweet

Always looking flawless
Every time we come to pass
She makes me second guess
Makes me break like glass

Scared of her beautiful cage
While trying to lock myself in one
See her performance's backstage
With perfection I am done

She is intimidating
Because of her public rating
I suppose the public may have lied
Forgot to tell what she can hide

To Be a Leader

They try so hard to fit in
Making each identical, a cruel cloned twin
While I fight hard to stay me
A closed door without a key

I would, could be
Something fantastic, something me
If only I stood up and said
The thoughts that whisper in my head

The choice is yours to make
Values are give or take
Leaders never fear attack
Ask now, what's holding you back?

REMEMBERING THE **F**UTURE

And I try to find the art
Of remembering the future
With only dividation and a feeling in my heart
The destination from nothing can deter

Remember when we were twenty eight
Yet write of it, still underage
I begin to feel it's already too late
Show is over before I'm on stage

Do we plan our plans neatly
Then forget to live them out
Looking forward to the future sweetly
The system I am beginning to doubt

REALITY

There's a limit to our lives
That tears at us like knives
Without it we could fly
Set the limit to the sky

Footprints

Only follow in the footsteps created
With nothing but sand between the toes
The path the stars have awaited
Which only the moon knows

A concrete path walked a thousand times
Is nothing against the trail that leads
Somewhere deep outside the given lines
Into the trees; onto the weeds

Follow in the footprint
Of the footprints not yet here
Create an original imprint
The next infamous shakespeare

Walk among the wildflowers
With stars caught in your hand
Splash in storms and rain showers
On the path to undiscovered land

WAY BACK NOW

And again I am here
Waiting just like then
As the years come ever near
Yet I still remember when,

I was alone forevermore
Then couldn't imagine going back
New people, new ever waiting door
The smile I now lack

All over again I sat here
Afraid of them, I could clearly see
Now I rest my self down in their chair
Wondering, would I be afraid of me?

FIREFLIES

What happened to the those days
When we were young
Our spirits were ablaze
Our stories still unsung

Our worst problems never compared
To the ones we are facing now
We never could have been prepared
For the things this future would allow

Endless nights of fireflies
And barefoot adventures in the wood
Blissfully ignorant, beautifully unwise
When we were running in the neighborhood

When did we draw that line
Growing up against our will
By our looks alone are we defined?
Age comes with sitting still?

Only when those days are gone
Will we remember what we need
Looking at the sky; laying on the lawn
Never, never grow up I plead

Soft as Rock

Silk smooth as water
Lilies and love
Princesses daughter
Pure as a dove

Wrists circled in gold
Velvet dresses and bows
Restraints that don't lose hold
Why does it matter what she knows

A beautiful face masks her power
Her quiet is confidence mistaken for shy
Conquering without force each hour
Intentions hidden beneath the eye

Rough hard as rock
Confusing as love
Not content to sit and talk
In this way, we rise above

DEEP MIRRORS

Deep in a mirror of black slivered glass
Thorns to her vibrant red rose
A whole other level, a brand new class
Of beauty which only she knows

The flaws scaring her face
And the scrape down her eye
Still strong, full of grace
Thriving, not withered or dry

A looking glass goes only so far
Never past the image, never past the skin
They want to know her, but see only scars
Ignored and alone, not fitting in

She in herself shines bright, not like the Sun
But a dark luminous light
Too afraid of the spotlight to be a star
A full shining disc of pure silver moon

A work of white canvas art
One which only the painter can scold
Past the layer of peeling paint she is smart
She is bold

Long past a mirror of black slivered glass
From thorns and hate she rose
To a whole new level, her very own class
A beauty everyone knows

Exceptional Fear

I am exceptional
Due to an unworldly mistake
Is talent mine to earn or keep
Or do I prosper on others fear of it

I introduce the whole new use
Of beautiful words and gifts
Then sit guilty as they now prosper
Jealousy and Heresy
I make.

Untapped talent I long to embrace
But halt knowing that
Afraid they might
Take my place

So much more they cannot
Imagine; my fear
Of their beautiful, effortless talent
Compared to my mistakes

Do we not praise the other
So our unearned glory will stay
Then live the lie we once knew true
Leaving the other, a greater person

I was exceptional
Due to my own mistake
Talent slipped through my open fingers
When they were no longer afraid

Freedom

A willow wood oak
Sticking out of a green grassland
No factory smoke
It was, this world, once grand

Clouds of pure white
Drape over sea green waves
We destroy with all our might
And strip all the jewels from caves

A chain fence restrains us as a child
Sunglasses made to block out the light
A scary thought, loving the wild
And nature is considered a fright

Tall golden untamed weed
Lay beyond the chain fence wall
Blocked off from precisely what we need
In a world as wide as ours, barriers are quite small

To them I suppose,
It's a frightening thing
For a plant to choose how it grows
Or a bird without tied down wings

Freedom is truly a wild thought
Untamed and unchecked; it is fire
That burns through chain and knot
Wild and free, this world was made to inspire.

Careless

Live your life like a game
Party all night, feel no shame
Take each day as a dare
Dance through them without a care

Hands thrown in the air
This attitude is quite rare
Instead, an overdose of work and pain
Feeds our need to complain

Be silly, impulsive, quick to fire
Those who enjoy it all, admire
No need to hide under a rock
Crushed by all the endless talk

Saddle the sun and tame the cloud
Life's a song, play it loud
Just keep laughing, this too shall pass
Be your own social class

DREAMS

It's a vivid image in a mind
With obstacles to tall to climb
Ends too far to ever meet
Make victory twice as sweet

Think the impossible
Reality is just an obstacle
Raise hands up to grab the stars
Footprints engraved on Mars

Once the world we knew was flat
Until someone questioned that
For all we know, we cannot fly
Until someone takes the sky

Thousand unreached goals in mind
Weighing down upon mankind
Each person's abandoned dream and goal
Leaves in us an empty hole

If not for lack of trying
Our inspiration is dying
It is long past time to light the flame
The lost dreams we must reclaim

Think of gone childish wonder
Not of soft rain, but of thunder
The power of a determined brain
Churns and quakes a hurricane

A Story
· · · · · · · · ·

Deep in the pages
Yellowed and torn
Lay a tale of old times
Danger, excitement, are born

Here lay a story
Full of heroes and more
And here lay a reader
Who is wise beyond their years
They wish to slay dragons
Wave a mighty wand
Or yet, to run from enemies
With satchel bag and knife

Lost away in story land
Where magic comes to glide
Huddled with their yellow pages
Quiet, yet wise

To be the one with the story,
A true hero of their kind
Lay there in silence, my reader,
And you shall get your time

One who drifts soundlessly
Seems meek and shy somehow
Yet could crush them with the truth
With the brave hero in their minds

Alas they wait
Deep in yellowed pages
Till pen meets paper; inking fate
Writing a tale to last the ages

Acknowledgements

Thank you to Fran Eiss, for helping me with the editing and answering many of my questions.

Thank you to all of my teachers, who are all equally inspiring.

Thanks to Katie Thekkekandam, for encouraging me to enter my first poetry contest.

Thank you to Kaylin Wright, for being the first person to read much of my poetry.

Thanks to all my friends, who are amazing,

Thanks to my neighbor, Mark Gilroy, who helped me with some final publishing details.

Many thanks to my family, who have been very supportive of my writing.

And thanks to you, the reader!

About the Author

Mia Guiliano lives in Brentwood, Tennessee with her family and two dogs. She enjoys reading, running, and painting in her spare time. This is her first wide-spread published work.

Find out more about Mia's writing on social media:
@Mia_Guiliano.writing

www.ingramcontent.com/pod-product-compliance
Lightning Source LLC
Chambersburg PA
CBHW071418290426
44108CB00014B/1876